THE ARTIST AS MYSTIC

THE ARTIST AS MYSTIC

Conversations with Yahia Lababidi

By Alex Stein

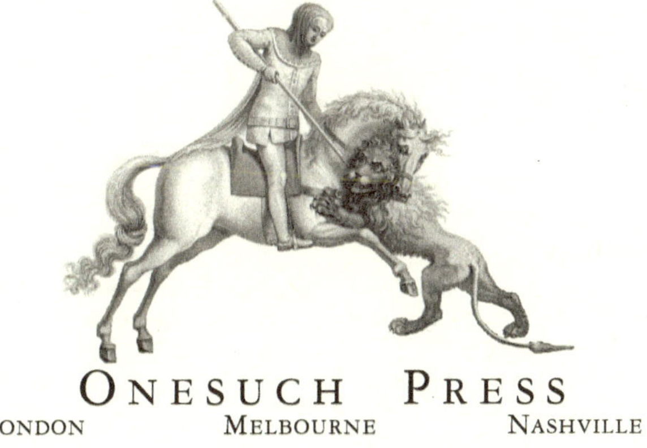

Onesuch Press

London Melbourne Nashville

A ONESUCH BOOK
Published by ONESUCH PRESS
PO Box 303BK, Black Hill 3350 Australia

National Library of Australia Cataloguing-in-Publication entry
Author: Stein, Alex.
Title: The Artist as Mystic : Conversations with Yahia Lababidi
Alex Stein, Yahia Lababidi.

ISBN: 978 0 9872760-4-9 (pbk.)
ISBN: 978 0 9872760-3-2 (ebook)

Subjects: Lababidi, Yahia.
Mysticism and art.
Spiritual life.
Private revelations.

Other Authors - Contributors:
Lababidi, Yahia.

Dewey Number: 701.08

The paper used in this publication meets the minimum requirements of ANSI/NISO Z39.48-1992 (R 1997) (Permanence of Paper). The paper used in this book is from responsibly managed forests.
Printed in the United States of America, the United Kingdom and Australia by Lightning Source, Inc.

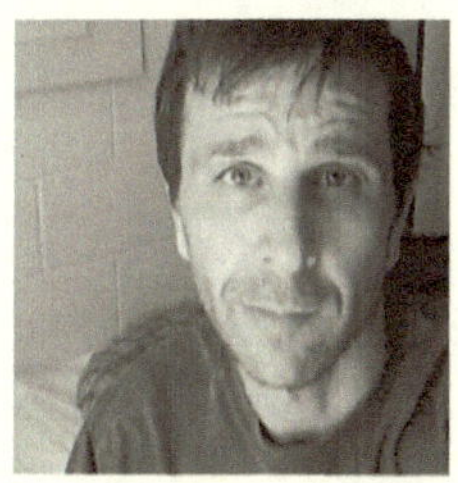

Alex Stein is an essayist, aphorist, and illustrator whose recent books include *Made-Up Interviews With Imaginary Artists* (Ugly Duckling Presse, 2009) and *Weird Emptiness* (Wings Press, 2007). He lives in Boulder, Colorado, and works at the University of Colorado's Norlin Library.

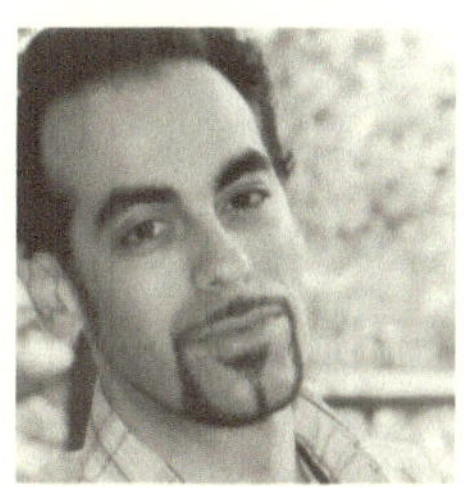

Egyptian-American **Yahia Lababidi** is an aphorist, poet, and essayist. He is the author of a new poetry collection, *Fever Dreams* (Crisis Chronicles Press), an essay collection, *Trial by Ink: From Nietzsche to Belly Dancing*, and a collection of aphorisms, *Signposts to Elsewhere* (Jane Street Press). Lababidi's work has appeared in several anthologies, and been translated into Arabic, Hebrew, Slovak, German, Spanish, Dutch, Swedish, Turkish, and Italian.

Contents

Preface

To ease me into this preface, Yahia has offered to build me "a little runway."

"That's all you need," he says, "just a little runway. Once you get airborne again, you'll remember how to fly."

The first thing he brings is a quotation from Sander L. Gilman's book *Conversations with Nietzsche: A Life in the Words of His Contemporaries.*

"Paul Ree was Nietzsche's friend and a fellow philosopher," says Yahia. "In his remembrance, Ree writes, 'Nietzsche was more important for his letters than for his books and even more important for his conversations than for his letters.'"

Conversation is the litmus test, I believe. Conversation is the pudding in which the proof resides. In conversation we give the most complete, up to date, version of ourselves. The newly minted along with the all but spent. In conversation, everything that is in reach of his tongue is available to the speaker: What he is; what he knows; what he can get away with.

"Yes," I tell Yahia, "I like that quote. It suggests that no one, not even Nietzsche, has an individual destiny more important than his communal destiny."

"I have another one," says Yahia, "but it is in Latin."

"Pig-Latin, I hope," says I.

"Mortui Vivos Docent," says Yahia. "It means, the dead shall teach the living."

"I like it," I say. In truth, I am overwhelmed. I can suddenly feel the moss of the grave growing on me.

"You don't have to like it," says Yahia.

"No," I say, "it's perfect."

**

In the course of "The Artist as Mystic: Conversations with Yahia Lababidi," there are three poems, that would otherwise have been spelled out in their full glory, that we chose to abbreviate to avoid copyright infringements. I speak of the poem *"Ars Poetica,"* by Czeslaw Milosz, a paean so exquisite it seems almost impossible that a human being, in or out of trance, could have written it; I speak of Baudelaire's infamous "To the Reader," translated by Robert Lowell in a white hot fury of lunatic affinity; and I speak of Stephen Mitchell's seminal and, to my taste, unmatched translation of Rainer Rilke's visionary "Archaic Torso of Apollo." In these cases, I have done what I was able, sometimes with a scalpel, sometimes with a sledgehammer, to reshape the poems for the purpose of fair usage, meanwhile retaining their essential sense and carriage. Otherwise, I stand by these conversations as intact to my deepest hearing. Just as I experienced them. All I can bring to any proceeding, anyhow, is my witness. Which must necessarily include my witness of myself.

***

Between us, Yahia and I refer to our conversations as

"lyric interviews" or "collaborations," but I have also heard Yahia call them "séances" and, at other times, "hallucinations."

Sometimes as I was working on the material that would become one or the other of these conversations, I could hear Yahia's voice very clearly inside my thinking, speaking out my thoughts. "Make every line count," the Yahia in my head would say, as if that had not been my maddening scruple ever since I determined my personal capacity and excavated my deepest ambition. Make every line count. Make every word matter. Do so by alchemy, by editing, with compassion, and under the strictest guidelines of conscience. Give yourself over to the passionate wherewithal of the creative moment. Make of your art an offering to the spirits (those "literary masters," as Yahia calls them) with whom you would commune.

****

One of my favorite poets, Bob Dylan, wrote "How many ears must one man have, before he can hear people cry?"

One is too many, three is not enough.

Fellow traveler on what Yahia calls "the great whale hunt through the mind-sea," this one is for you.

Alex Stein
Boulder, CO
May, 2012

The Prayer of Attention

Yahia believes the condition of the artist is exalted.
"Even if the artist lives in disregard?" I ask.
"Yes," Yahia insists.
"Even if he is scorned and impoverished?" I ask.
"Still, yes," says Yahia.
"What does that mean, then—exalted?" I ask.
"It means," says Yahia, "called to service."
"Oh," I say, a sinking feeling coming over me, "you mean that soldiery of light, that brigade, born to march into the Valley of the Shadow?"
"Yes," replies Yahia, "precisely!"

There is a moment in the life of Rimbaud when he comes to realize that he is a poet, but that it is not his fault. He writes: *"It is wrong to say, 'I think.' One has to say, 'I am thought.' I is another. Too bad for the wood that finds itself a violin."* For me, that tells all. I haven't studied the lives of the mystics as closely as I have the lives of the artists but I do see the correspondences. The life of the artist may not be apparently monastic, or holy, but there is the same sense of sacrifice, of vocation, of having been entrusted with something greater and dearer than one's own happiness. Imagine! To hold something more dear than one's own happiness. That cannot be a voluntary thing. We want, as much as we can, to be happy. Isn't this true? Yet, there are these strange, luminous creatures who recognize that there is something to which they must submit, in order to be fully realized. It is the wood finding itself a violin.

Kafka is another. Another artist as mystic. Another who recognizes this affinity. In his journal he writes *"This tremendous world I have inside of me. How to free myself, and this world, without tearing myself to pieces. And rather tear myself to a thousand pieces than be buried with this world within me."* Again, the calling. Again the gift slash curse privileged. The whole life structured toward developing the necessary faculties, the necessary conditions. Rimbaud must be drunk and whoring all the time, Kafka has literally to abstain and deny himself everything.

Might I be permitted one more quotation? Kierkegaard. He was another who saw his life very much as a sacrifice. *"A little pinch of spice,"* he writes in his journal. *"Here, a man must be sacrificed. He is needed to impart a particular taste to the rest."* He is just a concentrated fllavor, that is to say. He doesn't take it personally. In another place, he writes something to the effect that, a writer is lost when he confounds himself with what he has produced and ceases to think of himself as merely an instrument. All of these lives, all of these sometimes protracted convulsions of living, contain something of a renunciation, a continual giving up, or self-limiting, at their core.

I have sought such artists out, combed their thoughts for these instances, because, from very early on, they helped me to make sense of my own sometimes reluctant yearnings. Through them, I received confirmation and solace. In their lives and words I heard the echoes of my own submission to ideals that seemed at times almost too dauntingly resistant in despite to other possibilities.

I was 18 years old when I began to guess that I too might be a writer. The change stunned me. I had known myself one way and that knowing was silenced. I had been loud and cheap, interested in the noise of the world and in adding to that noise, and now I withdrew and began asking myself if there was a specific purpose to my being and if that purpose had to do with writing. I didn't want to have anything to do with anyone until I could figure out what was happening. Eventually I understood that I was never going to figure out what was happening. Some things, some people, some ways of living just fell away.

I was attending college in D.C. I went through several room-mates, almost without noticing them. I was absorbed with books, those dead friends who were telling me: "Come, let's go this direction, let's try this pathway..." The books were almost always accidental. I don't know how to say where they came from, except to quote from Rumi: "*What you are seeking is also seeking you.*" One led to another. A series of spirits come to try and draw my own spirit out.

Kafka was the first. I remember reading "A Hunger Artist." In total immersion, my long frame crouched, like a shadow or a gargoyle, against the wall of my dorm room. I didn't know then that Kafka was revising this as he lay dying and that it was a parable for his spiritually dissatisfied life, but it struck me, at 18, as the most profound encounter I had yet had with myself. You know the story, of course. No one is interested any longer in the hunger artist. Professional fasting has lost its cachet with the public. The hunger artist is wasting away, forgotten, in the dirty straw of a carnival cage. Weakened almost to the point of death by his fanatical pursuit, he is at last removed by the overseer, and his place taken by a vital, bright-eyed panther. *"I always wanted you to admire my fasting,"* the hunger artist tells the overseer. *"We do admire it,"* the overseer replies. *"But you shouldn't admire it,"* the hunger artist continues perversely, *"because I have to fast, I can't help it. It is just that I couldn't find the food I liked. If I had found it, I would have stuffed myself like you or anyone else."* That was the thought that undid me. That this spiritual food that one was craving simply could not be found. And that nothing else would do. Better to starve, then, says the hunger artist. Better to starve and to make of that starvation one's nourishment.

I thought of this transformation that I was undergoing, this shedding of old skin, as too private to explain to anyone. When I had to be around people who knew me as I had been, I hid. I put on the best mask I could find. I didn't know exactly what was happening. It looked like a kind of crisis, but it wasn't. Or, rather, it was, but it was a fruitful crisis. The only way I could explain it to myself, even, was in the composition of dialogs, monologs, parables and, finally—this was the form that gave me the most relief, that offered the deepest bloodletting—aphorisms. In the aphorism, I didn't have to say "I," I could just let the thing speak itself, so I didn't feel compromised or embarrassed or vulnerable. A shy truth that could also be a general truth. I wrote, *"The thoughts we choose to act upon define us to others. The ones we do not, define us to ourselves."* They had enough of an air of mystery and ambiguity that I could bring them out and not feel exposed. I wrote, *"Impulses we attempt to strangle only develop stronger muscles."* It was with these aphorisms that I understood—accepted!—that I was in it, and that it was real. I showed my aphorisms to more people than I should have. Some responded with arched eyebrows, some with indifference or incomprehension, but those who were close enough to me, my dear friends, lovers, or family, understood that I was confessing in code.

In the culture I come from, a saying is a magical thing. It was something people were always happy to hear or recite, and if I happened to have written it, that was good, too. I grew up with grandmothers, both maternal and paternal, who spoke almost exclusively, at times, in sayings. A string of proverbs. Sing-songy, witty-wise remarks. When I found myself writing such things, it made sense for me to share them. You share a saying. You quote a saying. They come in handy when you are tongue tied. My grandmothers' sayings were mostly commentaries on Love or the differences between men and women. Not sayings that necessarily spoke to me as a child, but the idea of speaking in sayings, and of generalizing out of particulars, stuck with me.

As I think of it now, it was Wilde who first turned me toward the territory that would inform my own aphorisms. I was 16 when I read "A Portrait of Dorian Gray." I stole the book from a classroom in my school because I liked the cover. It showed a ghoulish, aged face in a gaudy picture-frame. Standing next to it, locked into its gaze, it seemed, was a vital, sophisticated, exquisite dandy, bearing scarf and cane. I was interested in traditional horror stories at that time. I read…well, I read Stephen King. And 'Dorian Gray' was my point of transition. From physical horror, to spiritual horror, I suppose. I took the book home and read it through in one night. Then I read everything of Wilde's that I could get my hands on. I was writing already, but I wasn't yet writing truly. You know Kafka's line about literature being an axe for the frozen sea within us? The frozen sea within me was still very much frozen and I didn't mind that it was frozen. I liked it frozen. I skated happily upon it.

What impressed me in Wilde was his ability to play with serious subjects. To make light of them. I thought I could pick that quality up for myself. Throwing out, with seeming gaiety, a thought that was, at base, painful and dark. Born of real suffering and insight. Every part of Dorian Gray spoke to me. I highlighted almost the entire book. I underlined more passages than I left unmarked. I scribbled in the margins furiously. He said he was summing up the entirety of existence in a phrase. Anyway, he was summing up in a phrase the entirety of my existence. It was my first exposure to the philosophical concept of detachment. To become the spectator of one's life is to escape the suffering of life, he suggested. That hit me. I didn't know why, or how deeply, until a couple of years later, when I started working on my own detachment. It is this detachment, in its variety of permutations, that I admired in the lives of the artists whom I would eventually take for my models. This supreme indifference, even in the hardest of times, to one's own welfare. So long as one could pull off the alchemist's trick of turning it into art, it no longer mattered then how tortured the romance, how isolated the life, or how penniless the pocket. On the contrary, the more one gave up, the more authority was vested in the creation. The beauty lay in the tension between what one had surrendered in pursuit of the achievement and what had been achieved.

And then there was Nietzsche. I came upon his work in a college English class. There was no reason for him to be in that syllabus, but there he was. Those were the days when I would read and think without sleeping, sometimes for two or three days in a row, so that I could hold on to whatever intensity I was experiencing and magnify it. If I was reading and thinking and not sleeping, it was like rocks being struck together. Sparks would rise: ideas and aphorisms. I treated all of my reading at that time as if I were being granted audience with the writer and in order to honor that audience I had to come prepared. I had to be as attentive as possible, in order that I could sound the depths of that writer. In that way, too, I was learning to sound my own depths.

I first read "Thus Spake Zarathustra." I read it like a sleep-walker. I breathed it in. A shocked inhalation, almost unconscious. When I read it again, maybe a decade later, more intentionally, in the desert outside of Cairo, it was like a long slow exhalation that let me finally examine what I had received. I went to the desert periodically. Pilgrimages to empty and refill myself. On the occasion of my re-reading of Nietzsche, I was by the Red Sea, among mountains. I read 'Zarathustra' straight through. Every time I go to the desert it is with the intention and in the belief that I am going to encounter that part of myself that is not entirely accessible in other circumstances. In the desert, there is nothing to hide behind, no-where and no-one to turn to. It is where all those crazy hermits and mystics— my people!—had their visions. It's an extreme environment and I suppose I felt if I flirted with that extremity, but in a committed, honorable way, a breakthrough might be granted me. If you were somehow avoiding yourself and you went to the desert, then somehow you would meet. The rumblings of eternity were there, if you could just be still enough, quiet enough, and indifferent enough, to your self, to your many selves, to your many silly selves. So taking Nietzsche to the desert was a gesture toward meeting both him and the him-that-was-also-me in the same moment.

There in the desert, reading the lonely words of Nietzsche, I came to realize the necessity of that loneliness. Loneliness as prerequisite for the sublime sensations or epiphanies I sought. You could be alone around people, alone in your living room, but if you reached toward this elemental loneliness—alone with the sand, the rock, the water, the stars and the sea—than you could experience a deeper innocence and purity of perception, and as a result, become a better witness to the life inside you and around you. Nietzsche talks about "the price." And I understood that, there in the desert. The harsh loneliness of his life had given him the richness of himself. The desert is inhospitable. It doesn't really want you there. But, if you could stay there, if you could stick it out, you could be granted an access that you couldn't find anywhere else. There is a desert quality to Nietzsche's writing, I think. It doesn't care much for you. It may, perhaps, want you there, but it doesn't need you there. It doesn't seek to appease the reader. It is not eager to please. It wants only to declare its harsh, bold truths, and if you can stand it, you can stay.

Heidegger said something, on longing, that seems to me to sum up what I am trying to express here about the loneliness. For, after all, it is not the loneliness that matters, it is the longing. The loneliness is a side effect, a symptom of the longing. We are speaking of the artist as mystic. There was a longing in me that I didn't realize, that I couldn't understand, that Heidegger helped define: *"Longing is the agony of the nearness of the distant."* That got me. It seemed that it was right there. It! I could almost brush it with my fingertips. But it wasn't right there. I was trafficking with metaphysics, with mere hope, when in fact it was very far away. It was not mine. It was not within reach. Just that occasionally, for reasons unknowable, it came within reach. And when it did, everything was perfect and nothing else mattered or could matter. But it was not mine, this great, calming beauty. So of course I would lose it. Of course I would stumble. The agony of the nearness of the distant. That was it. That was the great thing I was groping toward, the great thing that the aphorisms, on occasion, brought me upon.

One more thing, before we finish. Every time I thought of this conversation that we were about to have, this one that we are now having, an image would recur in my mind. I kept trying to clarify to myself this idea of the artist as mystic, the artist and the mystic, and their disparate ways of summoning the spirit, and I kept coming back to the idea of attention. Attention is the artist's mode of prayer. Picasso speaks, for example, of taking off his shoes before entering his studio. Like Moslems do when they enter their mosques. That was his way of sanctifying his art. The artist prays through attention. I think of my dreams. I think of those times when I fly in my dreams. I think there must be some connection between how I fly in my dreams and this state I sometimes come to in writing when I feel that I am aloft, ecstatic. The thing I want to say: In my dreams, it is blinking that brings me down to the ground. When I blink, in my flying dreams, that is when I begin to fall. When I have fallen, I don't know how to get back into that state. But if there is a formula, I think it must have to do with attention. So long as you have your eyes open that flight is possible. Eternal vigilance is the price of freedom, someone has said. So long as one's eyes are open, wide open, there is that chance, again, that one will soar.

To Go and Seek the Twilight Hour

Introduction

Franz Kafka's blue octavo notebook aphorisms were first published in 1953, in the posthumous collection Preparations for a Country Wedding, under the heading "Reflections on Sin, Suffering, Hope, and the True Way." That header, with its stair-stepping triplet of independent clauses—Sin! Suffering! Hope!—and its deft note of plea, was one of the innumerable publicity tweaks that Max Brod, zealous agent of Kafka's literary estate, would perform on behalf of (or, some might say, in despite of) the spiritual reputation of his enigmatic friend.

It was Kafka who had culled the aphorisms initially from the pair of blue notebooks into which they had been handwritten. He transposed these, slightly editing some, onto consecutively numbered slips of paper he had arranged at his bedside.

Illness had set Kafka free. Tuberculosis had declared itself a month earlier when he first coughed up a little blood. Kafka would spend eight months, from September, 1917 to April, 1918, in Zurau, in the Bohemian countryside, at his sister Ottla's house. In a letter from that time, Kafka compared himself to the "happy lover" who exclaims: *"All the previous times were but illusions, only now do I truly love."*

Of this letter, the scholar Roberto Calasso has written: *"Illness was the final lover; which allowed him to close the old accounts."* Three days into his stay, Kafka scribbled: *"You have the chance if ever there was one, to begin again. Don't waste it."*

The sequence he produced was a first on many levels. It was, and would be, the only text in which Kafka directly confronted theological themes, and it marked the appearance, for him, of a new form.

> #52 *In the struggle between yourself and the world, hold the world's coat.*
>
> #53 *It is wrong to cheat, even if it is the world of its victory.*

Calasso also wrote that, *"Though Kafka made no surviving reference, either direct or indirect, to the existence of these aphorisms, one can't help but think that he meant to publish them in a form corresponding to the way he arranged them on those slips of paper."* In Calasso's edition of the now-fabled notebooks, the following aphorism, #109, concludes the aphorism sequence.

> *There is no need for you to leave the house. Stay at your table and listen. Don't even listen, just wait. Don't even wait, be completely quiet and alone. The world will offer itself to you to be unmasked; it can't do otherwise; in raptures it will writhe before you .*

Interestingly, this aphorism was one of eight that did not appear in either original notebooks. They were added by Kafka at a later time—possibly in 1920—and were demarcated from the aphorisms that preceded them by a quick stroke of the pen.

Part One: The Twilight Hour

Alex: What do you think is 'the world' of which Kafka writes in Aphorism #109? What do you make of what seems to be the slightly eroticized imagery with which it concludes? Could one call this aphorism pure sublimation? Simply the dream of an impotent? Where does one draw the line in looking to literary figures for answers or sustenance?

Yahia: Before anything else, 'the world' of which Kafka writes in this aphorism is a present moment that he, as a creative artist, happens to be alive to and, with that present moment, alive, as well, to its present possibilities. I think, also, that 'the world' of which Kafka writes in this aphorism is the 'there-world' into which he enters to write, as the yogis enter theirs to breathe. Do you know this story? Kafka has just written the most threadbare sentence possible, 'He looked out the window,' and having written such a sentence wrote immediately upon its heels, 'I know that it is already perfect.' Now, isn't that striking? That this nest of neuroses, this terribly insecure man, could write—could know!—'it is already perfect.' From where did this uncharacteristic confidence come? This sounded note of surety?

During his encounters with 'the world,' Kafka is no longer quite himself and his hand is being steadied. Just recently, a poet friend shared some Buddhist teachings, and one of the fables I think comes very close to what I am trying to express. The sun is always out there, he said, but we walk around with clouds above us, with their cloud shadows upon us. If we can slip out from beneath those clouds or if we can stretch up our arms and muck those clouds about a bit, the sun will shine upon us. The sacred world wants to shine upon us.

But where is it, this 'out there'? Where is it, this sacred 'there-world' to which we would go? I like the word interstice. A gap or a break in something generally continuous. A paradox, like the snake that swallows its own tail until it has swallowed itself entirely. A double-joint in time, or a space that is only a bit of fabric that gives, and one can just slip on through it. The interstate.

As a young reader, I envied the invalids. And the invalids spoke of their invalid status as enviable. Gibran and Proust, come to mind. Both were bed-ridden. Being bed-ridden was their permit to dream. It was a special dispensation, really, an exemption against engagement with the tedious responsibilities of the here-world. Invalidism gave them the license, and the luxury, to go 'there'. To go and seek the twilight hour.

Some invalids are life-long. Kafka probably romanticized himself so. Turned his affliction into a badge of honor. Proust once wrote that the neurotics have given us everything. They are the ones who have saved the world, created the world, made the world worthwhile. Invalidism eased Kafka of the burden of himself. Eased him of the chattering fears that told him, 'You must do better!' That told him, "It will always be beyond your abilities, whatever you choose."

I have been thinking, too, of fairy tales. The idea of Alice and the rabbit hole and its connection with physics. I don't know much about physics. I'm just another artist-groupie, but I am captivated by the idea of a wormhole. A hypothetical tunnel connecting disparate points in light-space, with the attendant, hypothetical, possibility of time travel. None of this is encouraged by hard science, but neither is it entirely refuted. Disputed, more-like. This idea of a shortcut between worlds, which, for me, translates as a shortcut into creative space, where inspiration is able to move with more agility and vision to engage with more dexterity. The world down the rabbit hole. One moment you are in the here-world and the next you are in the there-world. But, how? That is the crazy part. How does one devise a way of getting there? Or at least how does one devise a way of not blocking oneself from getting there?

As a teenager I read The Lion, The Witch and the Wardrobe, the first volume in C.S. Lewis's "Chronicles of Narnia." Before, I had read only horror genre literature. The Lewis book worked for me brilliantly on the level of pure horror, and then it went much further. As a teenager, I wasn't aware of Narnia's sacramental undercurrents. Or that Lewis was a 'Christian Apologist' (as he has been dubbed) and Aslan a sacrificial Christ figure. None of that holy apparatus was relevant to me then, but it is relevant to me now. I return to the book both for scholarship and for Narnia. I like the idea of a closet, that eponymous 'wardrobe', through which the children can only sometimes gain access to Aslan, who is Narnia. I like how it shows that the wormhole experience cannot be forced. It loves to happen, perhaps, but its ways are inscrutable. One moment it is fur coats in a rickety wardrobe, but push a little harder, it becomes fir trees in a snowy forest, satyrs, fauns, and all possibilities.

I have a poem that describes something like this:

My hours are afraid of my days
mistrust placing their feet down
suspicious of finding a foothold
tick-tock they tip-toe self-consciously

My days are afraid of my years
never able to forget themselves
standing around as I try to sleep
shifting their weights, shuffling fears

In the interstices, it is timeless
unwound and happily unfound
there we slip through the sieve
between those immeasurable spaces.

That's really where it all is. Between those immeasurable spaces. The crazy part is getting there.

Part Two: The Repressed, Deviously, in Masquerade

Yahia: Kafka wrote many poems, but he did not call them poems. *There is no need for you to leave the house. Stay at your table and listen. Don't even listen, just wait. Don't even wait, be completely quiet and alone. The world will offer itself to you to be unmasked; it can't do otherwise; in raptures it will writhe before you.* This is an aphorism constructed of mystic stations. One might call it a prose fragment or bit of wandering mage come to roost. I myself have no objection to calling it a poem. But specifically it is an aphorism constructed of mystic stations. Like stations of the cross. When I read *There is no need for you to leave the house. Stay at your table and listen,* I think of Pascal's precept, that all our difficulties arise our inability to sit quietly in a room, alone. That if one could be still enough, if one could endure one's own company, if one could remain present. If only one could. If only. Kafka is addressing our tendency to flinch. We flinch, for self-preservation, when we are with ourselves too long, because it quickly becomes too much. The boredom, the suffering, the restlessness. *Don't even listen, just wait,* he says. Then, immediately: *Don't even wait, be completely quiet and alone.* He is a reluctant Messiah, our Franz. Distrustful of his own authority. He must immediately make qualifications, equivocate. He bids us 'wait'. Then, backpedaling hurriedly, insists: *Don't even wait, be completely quiet and alone.* Because even the most modest expectation might scare it (the 'there-world') away.

We sometimes strain for feeling as though sitting outside a foxhole with our guns, waiting for a fox. The fox never leaves. It will never leave. Because it knows it is being hunted. Watched-for. Expected.

Those lines, *'The world will offer itself to you to be unmasked; it can't do otherwise; in raptures it will writhe before you…'* bring me goose bumps and, yes, tears and, yes, I do think a sublimated eroticism is partly accountable for the charge, the zap. I think of Nietzsche, especially in Zarathustra, *'the waves are heaving breasts,'* etc. That from a man who may have seen all of one pair throughout his adult life. In a letter to Milena, Kafka will write: *To try and catch in one night, by black magic, hastily, heavily breathing, helpless, obsessed, to try and obtain by black magic what every day offers to open eyes!*

Alas, poor Milena! Imagine being the recipient of such a letter, imagine being a young woman learning about her young man, and receiving such a letter. How could it not sting? And imagine being the one who had sent such a letter. Imagine being the young man. How can such a letter ever be lived down? It is too big to regret. It is Van Gogh's ear. It is too much to take back. It is yesterday's moon. Sometimes a voice out from the chaos of spirits cries and one finds oneself having written. Can one say that? Or perhaps it is only poetry. The young man, in fear of the young woman, writing of sack-cloth and ash, wishing his body would be burnt away. Nothing more to it. Whatever is dammed must find another outlet. Whoever is damned must find another heaven.

The Ecstatics from my tradition, the Persian tradition, could be wildly erotic, but because they were addressing themselves to God they felt safe. For Kafka, the mystic ritual he called 'writing' was his safe zone. Where he could let it all out and breathe light like a spirit fish swimming between stars. Mysticism is desire, like everything else is, and the desire of mysticism is a flaming arrow launched toward union. That union of the mystic, fire reaching to fire, no less than any carnal union, is an erotic experience. An ecstasy in the specifically Greek sense of ekstasis, meaning 'outside oneself.'

Part of what we read in Kafka is too personal. Tedious neurasthenic considerations. Documents for the doctors at the Sanitarium of Hypochondria. The repressed, finding its way, surfacing, deviously, in masquerade. And part of what we read in Kafka is a universalized, lived, sensuality. Shy experience of the self as other. Veiled encounters with the beloved. Butt-naked tusslings. And why not? To get there means 'union', long longed-for (or, it may be, 'reunion,' long hoped for) and it induces bliss. The 'impotent' who eroticizes the world, for me, he is the prophet. And I'm not the only one who thinks this. Lawrence Durrell, in his novel Justine, writes, *"the sick men, the solitaries, the prophets [!]...all who have been deeply wounded in their sex."* The statement lacks proportion, but there is truth in it. To be wounded in that way is to dam a furious river that begins, as Rilke tells us, *'in the sky.' 'Making music is another way of making babies,'* writes Nietzsche. And yes that is sublimation and yes it does color thought, but doesn't it color thought in wonderfully feverish flesh tones and isn't all that fleshly frailty and failing a living part of Kafka's meaning for us—a necessary aspect of its divinity? Isn't all that partly its sacrament? And isn't the chaos and aren't the death-thralls just autumn leaves in their season?

As for your last question: Where does one draw the line in turning to these literary figures for answers or sustenance, or for that matter tips on elegant living?

Where does Kafka end and literature begin? Would I read Kafka's unpublished journals? Yes. Would I read Kafka's laundry list? Yes. Where does one draw the line? At what he agreed not to burn? I am with Max Brod. Everything Kafka wrote (or for that matter said or did) is interesting because whatever he does, he is still doing the work. And the work is just self-work, but so, too, could be said of anything any of us do, in any capacity, fence-mending, love-making, book-binding, that it is just self-work. With Kafka we are given the opportunity to witness a self-work master-technician seeking, with elegant precision, his own hinterlands, focused in a state of such contained urgency, that it is almost a trance of clairvoyance . Kafka is us, without the lying.

Shouldn't that change the way I read him? It should. And it does. It ups the volume on everything. Even if he only clears his throat, it rings like thunder. Because the fact of the matter is he has something thunderous in him to say, and the fact of the matter is we know that he does. That is the point. Some of this stuff, sure, it can be more navel gazing, more convolutions, but what we cannot fail to recognize in Kafka is that this is a guy who is wrestling with his angel, and that commands our attention. What he is up against, so are we up against.

In the two slender notebooks, those two blue octavo notebooks, meant for school-children, we get his private conversations. And in private conversations all of us tend to think more childishly, more innocently, more directly, about hope and suffering, good and evil. If Kafka were to have translated those private conversations into public fictions or such-like, something that could have been folded twice and shot skyward under cloak of literature, his style would have to have been necessarily more self-conscious, more ambiguous. But, because these were entirely private conversations, and because they were left so, they became perfect mirrors. Looking glasses. Beyond the fairy tale of the bardic. Verging on the estate of the vatic.

Listen, now: Aphorism #16: *A cage went in search of a bird.*

That's all of it. That's all there is. No root. No soil. Bloomed in thin air. Sometimes from Kafka, we get a truth that just is. A white, as it were, flower lapel that is not worn in irony.

That cautionary reprobate Charles Baudelaire once wrote, "*The greatest wile of the devil is to convince us that he does not exist.*" This echoes many of Kafka's octavo notebook aphorisms about the idea of evil. It's almost the cleric or the choir boy in Kafka writing at such times. At another level, though, it is as if he is some august theologian, transmitting a soul-map in code.

On this occasion, Yahia and I had intended to discuss Baudelaire. Along one line of literary thought, it goes: Kafka, Baudelaire, Nietzsche, Rilke. We had already discussed Kafka, so now we were on to Baudelaire. Except, when I asked Yahia where he meant to begin in Baudelaire, he said "with Bataille," which gave me a shudder.

Him and me, both, actually.

YAHIA: I stumbled across an interview with Georges Bataille, perhaps the only existent video recording of this strange creature speaking. He was being interviewed regarding his book called Literature and Evil. I'd read a little of his work. His study of Nietzsche and a couple of novels, but I was not aware of Literature and Evil and, before this video, I had never even see a photograph of him. But here he was, this shifty, shifting creature who looked as though he could be anything from a pedophile to a mass murderer.

The conversation on Bataille's side addressed writing as a form of evil and it shocked me to hear this man who has been referred to as a *"a metaphysician of evil,"* this transgressive writer obsessed with necrophilia and human sacrifice, talking in prim tones about literature, the entire project, being inseparable from evil. He calls writing the opposite of working and says that writers who make it their living are guilty. Guilty, at the minimum, of practicing hoo-doo, of dabbling in the black arts.

When the interviewer asks Bataille to give examples of his assertion, Bataille matter-of-factly reports the names of Kafka and Baudelaire. It is obvious, he says, that they are both on the side of evil. Baudelaire actually admits as much by calling one of his verse collections "Les Fleurs du Mal," "The Flowers of Evil." Making proud advertisement of his affiliation. And Kafka? Kafka's writings reveal a guilty conscience and that guilt is evidence enough. .

Literature, Bataille continues, is a childish pleasure.

The writer is the naughty boy, disobeying his parents who want him to earn a respectable living. By disobeying his parents and pursuing literature, the writer remains the naughty boy, until he becomes the immature adult, and then of course the slothful practitioner of an evil way.

At this point, the interviewer turns the focus back onto Bataille and asks, *"You've written about eroticism, what about that? Is there an infantile character to eroticism as well?"* *'The writer of eroticism,'* Bataille replies, *'is a child seeking punishment, because he knows that he is wrong. He is fascinated by a forbidden game and he is constantly afraid, and he must go further and further, hoping to be caught, because his shame has become intolerable.'* The Bataille who utters these words looks quite disturbing, and disturbed, and as I am hearing them I am also remembering a passage from his novel, Blue Noon, in which the narrator is masturbating beside his mother's corpse.

The only hopeful interpretation Bataille will offer comes toward the end of the interview. He says, *'Even though evil and literature are inseparable, perhaps because it forces us to confront the worst in ourselves—the very worst, because literature is that, the very worst in the human project—literature encourages us to look for ways to change ourselves.'*

So, he doesn't write literature off entirely. It's dangerous, he says. But it does shed some light.

ALEX: Tell me about Baudelaire.

YAHIA: I have been reading his intimate journals, which he calls, "My Heart Laid Bare." It was a title he took from Edgar Poe (as he was still then occasionally called) who said that any man who dared lay his heart bare would produce a work that was necessarily a masterpiece. This daring is the seed of a project that Baudelaire takes on during the last four or five years of his life, when he is ruined, physically, spiritually, and financially. It is a seed that will bear yet another strange flower. He has left Paris, and since it is Baudelaire, you know it must be in disgrace and misfortune. He is living in Belgium and he despises everything that Belgium stands for. One of the journals ongoing epithets, if someone is stupid, or if something is beneath him: *"It's the Belge!"* he will snarl. *"It has the Belge temperament!"* He is not in a good mood. He is not in a good situation. These are the conditions under which he is writing. These journals are home to a viper.

But, these same journals are also home to a broken-hearted man reaching out for salvation. Home to a man who can write, and mean it: *"My humiliations have been the grace of God."* Home to a man who had the misfortune, misperceived as the audacity, of becoming Modern before the age had become.

Alex, the journal progresses, contradictions heap upon contradictions, proliferate, and multiply. Selves multiply. This tortured man, who sees in everything its opposite, this tortured man, who tortures himself for pleasure, this tortured man who finds himself standing in opposition to his age, this tortured soul hearing voices getting louder. *"If a poet,"* he writes, *"demanded from the State the right to have a few bourgeois in his stable, people would be very much astonished, but if a bourgeois asked for some roast poet, people would think it quite natural."*

Baudelaire is forever engaging in argument, making a demonstration, asserting a point of order, even when he is at his most gregarious and self-revealing. The problem with an argument, though, in which one is engaged on both sides, on several sides, in fact, it quickly becomes unmanageable. One side must win and soon. The issue must be resolved, and soon. *"There is, in the creation of all sublime thought, a nervous concussion which can be felt in the cerebellum."* writes Baudelaire. The journals were meant to resolve things for once and for all, one way or the other, but the proliferating selves just kept on keening. They kept positing more and more contradictory circumstance, against every invention, until the drama, begun in deep noble yearnings, becomes, finally, heartbreaking, desperate, and pathetic.

Baudelaire never outgrows this project. He cannot even outlast it. The project was to have transformed him. He had transformed himself radically on other occasions . He was a Mama's boy who became a scandal. That's quite a leap right there. But before the efforts of the intimate journals, he had always transformed himself within the bounds of poetry and within the bounds of a well considered vanity. He had never attempted transformation on such a cosmic scale. *"To become a hero and a saint,"* he writes. He doesn't outgrow his project and he won't outlive it. He slips out the other way, into madness, bowing before his own reflection in the mirror. He can no longer recognize himself. In order to sign his name, he must copy it off the cover of one of his books because he no longer remembers how to spell it.

ALEX: Which edition are you using? The one with the picture of the poet on the cover looking gaunt, and hawkish, and fevered, and visionary? Or the one with the picture of the poet on the cover, looking flat-faced, with eyes like two round worlds, illuminated in space?

YAHIA: My edition begins with a preface by the translator, Christopher Isherwood.

ALEX: Well, tell me about that, then.

YAHIA: The preface makes a neat biographical summary, for those who don't know Baudelaire well, or his work, but want to get instantly at the heart of him. "*What kind of a man wrote this book?*" Isherwood begins. "*A deeply religious man, whose blasphemies horrified the orthodox. An ex-dandy who dressed like a condemned convict. A philosopher of love who was ill at ease with women. A revolutionary, who despised the masses. An aristocrat who loathed the ruling class. A minority of one. A great lyric poet.*"

That's Isherwood. I would have simply called him a whirlwind of polarities, a thinker whose thoughts are a storm of contradictions, and left it at that.

On re-reading the journals this time, for one reads them differently each time one returns, I got the sense of a man looking out over the edge of his life into the realm of total loss. This possessed soul who, a 150 years after he wrote, some still consider the most gifted lyric poet ever to lift a pen in a fog of hashish smoke and hear the voices of devils and angels dissecting art, and who still others consider even one of the most gifted lyric poets ever to lift a pen, period. This star-sent seer, by the journal's end, is so depleted of his promise and his possibilities, that he is pleading insatiably to God (and to Poe, as well) for intercession, in a language that would have sickened his younger self: "*Give me the necessary strength,*" he writes, "*to fulfill all my appointed tasks and grant my mother a sufficient span of life in which to enjoy my transformation."*

His mother, no less! He is like a man trying to balance on the cutting edge of a blade. He prays in contradiction as others pray in doubt.

Inside Baudelaire there is a creature he calls, 'the dandy.' The dandy is not entirely pleasant. It is not only that the dandy is concerned about his appearance and must live and wake and sleep before the mirror, but he is contemptuous toward everything—toward professions, toward women, toward other men of letters, toward love, sex, humanity. He is a malevolent being whose justification is his genius. *"Anyone is permitted to speak of themselves, provided they are amusing,"* the dandy writes, preening like a peacock. At that one, of course, even Oscar Wilde would have smiled. But after a while, the part of dandyism that is pure self-regard, however charmed, becomes puerile, because it does not lead onward. It always returns to itself. *"When I have inspired universal horror and disgust, I shall have conquered solitude,"* writes the dandy. And: *"There are only two places where one pays for the right to spend: women and public latrines."*

Enough, one wants finally to say of every cleverness, however clever it is. Enough of knowing everything. Now, use that knowing to change yourself. In a certain light, one can almost prefer the journal's passages that ache with sincerity. One can almost forgive them the grossness of their sentimentality—because they are arrows and because they are directed Out There. *"How many have been the presentiments and signs,"* he writes, *"sent me already by God that it is high time to act, to consider the present moment as the most important of all moments and to take for my everlasting delight my accustomed torment, that is to say, my work!*" He writes: "*To put my trust in God…to offer, every evening, a further prayer, asking God for life and strength…— to obey the strictest principles of sobriety, the first being the abstinence from all stimulants whatsoever.*"

Where-be your jibes now, Charles, your gambols, your songs?

ALEX: Speaking of Wilde, it was he who wrote, "*There is a fatality about good resolutions, in that they are always made too late.*" What comes after the preface in your edition?

YAHIA: After the preface, there is an introduction by T.S. Eliot. Eliot considers himself indebted to Baudelaire. One of Baudelaire's textual progeny. Without Baudelaire, Eliot is inconceivable, even to Eliot. Baudelaire thinks himself progeny of a more essential order. Thinks his own spirit literally a continuance of Poe's spirit. In 1860, replying to a letter of inquiry from the critic Armand Fraisse, he writes: "*….believe me if you will, I found poems and short stories which I had conceived, but vaguely and in a confused and disorderly way, and which Poe had been able to organize and finish perfectly.*"

Eliot does not go that far. He does not have to. Intellectual affinity is enough for the judicious Thomas Stearns. "*[Baudelaire's] technical mastery,*" he writes, "*can hardly be overpraised…[and] has made his verse an inexhaustible study.*" Their ideas about influence, that is to say, differ, but the Manna of influence acts on both poets in the same way, moderating an extensive inheritance (for Baudelaire from the estate of Poe, for

Eliot from the estate of Baudelaire) of ideas, of intonations, of territories, of imagery.

Baudelaire continues Poe. Feels literally to be breathing him out. The journals are undertaken upon Poe's direct provocation. In 1853, Baudelaire writes his mother: *"Now do you understand why, in the midst of the frightful solitude which surrounds me, I have understood Edgar Poe's genius so well, and why I have written so well about his wretched life?"*

The air around Baudelaire as he writes is dense with spirits. Messengers come to him, some from the realm of Poe and others from the realms of menace, while Eliot soberly accedes to the influences of Baudelaire at the craft level and at the level of language and atmosphere, and for the clarity, if not the soundness, of the delivery. (What we might call the style). The air around Eliot as he writes is serene, and at his right hand instead of a hash pipe, he has the maxims of Rochefoucauld.

Without Baudelaire, Eliot is inconceivable. Indeed, without Baudelaire, modern poetry would be something else. What that else would have been, who knows? Perhaps a rash of some kind. Perhaps the Eternal Rose. Without Baudelaire there would be a whole different history to the project of modernism. Think of that. A whole other history of celebrated names, poured over in celebrated scholarly treatises. Wither Rimbaud, if Baudelaire had never been? Wither Proust? Wither the Old Possum, himself, if the one who wrote the evil verses had never been?

ALEX: And this is in Eliot's introduction, you say?

YAHIA: No, sorry, that was me. Eliot writes, *"All first*

rate poetry is occupied with morality: this is the lesson of Baudelaire." He writes of Baudelaire as *"a deformed Dante,"* and finds in Baudelaire a *"theological innocence."*

"It was as though he was discovering Christianity for himself," writes Eliot.

The poets are connected most famously in ink through Eliot's recycling, into "The Wasteland," of some of lines from "Les Fleurs de Mal." Including the line *"Unreal City, under the brown fog of a winter dawn,"* adapted from, "Les Sept Vieillards." If one had a dog in the fight, one could argue, subjectively, but compellingly, that more or less obfuscated Baudelaire-ian influences are there in the poem more often than they are not there. I even recently read a postulation that the swan, in Baudelaire's "Le Cynge," who *"by the bank of a dry stream, on a dusty ground, waits vainly for rain"* is *" like the inhabitants of The Wasteland…[who are] all exiles, deprived of the true life."*

ALEX: Doesn't Eliot also use Baudelaire's line about the hypocrite reader?

YAHIA: I'm glad that you brought that up. I didn't want to mention it. Yes, at the end of the opening section of "The Wasteland" Eliot writes, *"You!—hypocrite lecteur!—mon semblable—mon frère."* A quotation from Baudelaire's preface to "Les Fleurs de Mal."

ALEX: Why didn't you want to mention that?

YAHIA: Because I have the poem here with me, and I would have wanted to recite from it.

ALEX: Well, it is one of the most confrontational lines

of poetry ever written, we might as well see how Baudelaire arrived at it.

YAHIA: In the Robert Lowell translation it reads:

Among the vermin, jackals, panthers, lice,
gorillas and tarantulas that suck
and snatch and scratch and defecate and fuck
in the disorderly circus of our vice,
there is one more ugly and abortive birth.
Which is, "BOREDOM."
You know it well, my Reader. This obscene
beast chain-smokes yawning for the guillotine—
you—hypocrite Reader—my double—my brother!

This poem is a hellish pantheon. A gallery of the grotesque. All the vices and then some are paraded and accounted for. But, even more terribly, the poet ends this degraded tour by saying we are all implicated. That you and I are partners with him, in this creation. This is Baudelaire hitting his nasty stride. This is Baudelaire with his chin up, and those terrible, piercing eyes, unflinching, looking back at us through the mirror of his verse.

"Hit the nail on the head, that time, didn't I?" he seems to be saying. "Cry No all you want, but my dark powers of penetration tell me you mean Yes."

Part Two: Neurasthenia

Yahia: Baudelaire refers to himself as a 'neurasthenic idler.' For variation, he sometimes uses the term 'acedia,' meaning 'malady of the monks.' An inability, at times, either to work or to pray. A paralysis of the will. He is always wrestling this paralysis. It is difficult to move, it is nearly impossible to care.

Neurasthenia projects symptomatically as fatigue, anxiety, depression. The word was coined in 1869. At the time it was perceived as resulting from stresses due to urbanization. There is an entry in which Baudelaire writes, *"If, when a man has fallen into habits of idleness, of daydreaming, of sloth, putting off his most important duties continually until tomorrow, another man were to awaken him with heavy blows of a whip and were to whip him unmercifully until he who was unable to work for pleasure now worked for fear, wouldn't that man, the chastiser, be his benefactor and truest friend?"*

This is what things have come to. He wants to be whipped. He feels that his sanity is at stake, his life, and his soul. The journals are emphatic. Plaintive. Weepy. Full of urgencies that all but pin the poet to the bed while he sleeps, and that hound his waking. *"To work from six o'clock in the morning, fasting at mid-day. To work blindly, without aim, like a madman. I believe I stake my destiny upon hours of uninterrupted work,"* he writes.

Maybe Bataille had the answer. However vile this stuff gets, however depraved, we are lucky to have it. It confronts the worst in us and it does so in every way that good literature can, brilliantly, thornily, furiously.

ALEX: That passage about being whipped reminds me of Kafka.

YAHIA: Does he remind you of Kafka? Last time you and I spoke of how Max Broad had published Kafka's notebook aphorisms under the heading, "Sin, Suffering, Hope, and the True Way." That marquee could hang above Baudelaire's intimate journal aphorisms, just as candidly. They are not entirely dissimilar writers, these two, nor entirely dissimilar thinkers. Both compress thought rapidly, are compelled toward compressed expression. Sometimes to the seeming detriment of readability. Baudelaire writing in compressed expression's more traditional medium, poetry, and Kafka in its less traditional medium, dream-prose. Both have interior lives like other people go to the theater. The serious theater, I suppose I mean. Both have imaginations that could be called visionary. Oh, believe me, between any two artists there are more similarities than there are differences, and between these two it was probably just the matter of their fates that distinguished them at all. Kafka in the gloom of pre-fascist Prague, and Baudelaire idolized in the dissipated streets of Paris, for a few glowing years, came to their similarities from opposite ends of experience. *"Now that my ladder's gone,"* as Yeats puts it, *"I must lie down where all ladders start, in that foul rag and bone shop of the heart."* The more you look at any two great artists, up close, side by side, the more the affinity. Here, Kafka writes: *"The Messiah will come only when he is no longer necessary."* And, here, Baudelaire: *"It would perhaps be pleasant to be alternately victim and executioner."*

Both are 'wounded in the sex.' to go back to a quote we used in the last interview. Both evince symptoms of sex recoil. Baudelaire came to the recoil only after the giantess and the dwarves and the debauch and the whoring, but come to it he did, while Kafka seems to have come to the recoil in advance of any but the most limited sexual experience, almost entirely by deduction.

Baudelaire's sex recoil was like a compound fracture of that bone, in the body, called Hope. He writes: "*The more a man cultivates the arts, the less he fornicates, and the more and more apparent the cleavage occurs between spirit and brute. To fornicate is to aspire to enter another, and the artist never emerges from himself.*" And then, this terse revelation: "*We make love with our excretory organs.*"

ALEX: So, love is always tainted, if love is even possible.

YAHIA: Yes. Something must have happened to Baudelaire in 1862. Five years before his death. A crisis. "*I have cultivated my hysteria with delight and terror and today I have received a singular warning,*" he writes. "*I have felt the wind of the wing of madness pass over me.*" With this, Baudelaire has become authentically frightened, and we who wish to, may now, in kindness, and in kindness to ourselves as well, begin to pity him and to consider, again, the conditions under which he was writing. The poetry is of a different order, it is always open season on the poetry, but, let us be a little gentler with the intimate journals. They were, after all, not edited for public viewing. He left them behind, mad, mute, stricken, when he left them.

ALEX: But he hasn't left them yet.

YAHIA: No, he has. We haven't. It's around the five-years-left-of-his-sanity mark that he moves to Belgium. That's around 1862. His publisher is bankrupt, his work has been judged obscene and is being suppressed, he is vain and no one to return his gaze, he is miserably poor, and now he has penned three of the greatest tribute lines ever offered to insanity (*"the wind of the wing of madness,"* indeed) and he is waiting for the axe to fall.

He can still write: *"Glorious empires may be founded upon crime and noble religions upon imposture."* And: *"In every man there are two allegiances, to God and to Satan; to climb higher, and to delight in descent and animality."* He can still write sensitively, and with the authority of one still enmeshed, of the paradox of desire, but where is the beloved who would receive it? All about him, only the dull-faced 'Belge', and their plodding incomprehension. First, a castle of emptiness, then a whole world of emptiness, and finally a universe of emptiness, is building itself around him, gradually cutting all else out.

Part Three: Spirit-Birds

Yahia: Since childhood, Baudelaire has had what he calls "a tendency to mysticism." *"Nothing upon the earth,"* he writes, *"is interesting, except religions."* I don't remember having seen this passage the first time I read the journals. It stunned me to see it on this occasion. As if it had been fresh planted there, just for my eyes. It seemed to suggest another way through. It seemed to open out into a territory left almost wholly unexplored, hitherto, by the poet. *"My humiliations,"* he writes in another place, *"have been the graces of God."*

Holy Saint Augustine! Could it have been otherwise?

Alex: Could it have been otherwise?

Yahia: It could have been otherwise. That is the unimpeachable sadness of the biography. He could have been otherwise. He cheated himself of himself—of "the other one," to use a Borges phrase, the Baudelaire who might have been—in order to play the prideful mutineer and to posture in that dilapidated theater house called The Streets of Paris.

I'm now going to read a poem by Czeslaw Milosz. He titled it 'Ars Poetica?' I think it should be titled, 'Address to Baudelaire in the Afterlife.' 'Ars Poetica?' is 36 lines, total, composed in 4 line stanzas. I'm going to read just 20 lines, including the 8 that conclude the poem.

As I am reading, I am imagining this as addressed to Baudelaire in the afterlife. You, though, may listen as you please.

Alex: I appreciate that.

[Here, Lababidi reads Milosz's "Ars Poetica" aloud. I

transcribe only a few lines. *"In the very essence of poetry there is something indecent,"* it begins. *"A thing is brought forth which we didn't know we had in us."* Somewhere in the middle there is a line that reads, *"What reasonable man would like to be a city of demons?"* and the poem concludes, almost rapturously, that one can only hope *"good demons and not bad, choose us for their instrument."*—A.S.]

When you are talking about Baudelaire, you are not talking about a reasonable person. But, think of it from the poet's perspective. If by *"be a city of demons"* Milosz means: allowing oneself to be possessed by spirit birds in endless variations, would it be so unreasonable for someone to make that choice? To choose to be a dwelling place of spirit-birds, if the alternatives were too painful to bear? If it were either a dwelling place of spirit-birds or nothing-at-all? Your honor? Ladies and gentlemen of the jury? I ask you.

It could have been otherwise. Baudelaire could have been otherwise. His sustained commitment to revolt was wasteful of his gifts, and took far more from him than he could afford to give. To what might a concurrent sustained commitment along some scholarly line have brought him? What if he had followed his childhood inklings and made a sidelight of the one thing, "religions," he would admit, when all else was gone, still interested him? And, purely from the point of view of self-preservation, wouldn't the pursuit of some accredited pastime have at least acted as a veil behind which the poet could have kept a secret of his malice and pride and so, perhaps, kept a place for himself in society? Where is the common sense? Did the genius kill it? Sartre wrote of Baudelaire that his greatest creation, and his greatest failure, was his personality. It's just a personality, after all, and nothing to get worked up over. Certainly nothing to get attached to.

ALEX: There is a children's story in which a young girl wants so badly to win a footrace that she goes to a witch and gets magic shoes. The young girl wins the race but she can't stop running. The shoes are wearing her. She runs and runs—she is run and run—until she dies from exhaustion.

YAHIA: Yes, this is the story of Baudelaire. His rebellion began to wear him. His personality became his interior reality. His exhaustion became his impetus.

ALEX: But, you say it could have been otherwise. Could Baudelaire have become the kind of mystic that you and I think of when we think of the word mysticism? Rilke, Rumi, Saint Paul? That kind of mystic? If he had grown old and left poetry behind? Don't you think he was bound to do that, if he lived, to leave poetry behind?

YAHIA: It's nice to think of Baudelaire in that Pantheon. But, Rilke, Rumi, Saint Paul….and Baudelaire? He, obviously, doesn't belong. Whether or not he would have, had he outlived his madness, that is a different story. He might have ended up an ecstatic. Other extremists have come to their revelations by that route. *"The road of excess leads to the palace of wisdom,"* Blake wrote. And Baudelaire, himself, in his supremely self-confident early prose wrote: *"Be drunk! On wine, poetry, or virtue, as you wish, but be drunk."* Which is not so dissimilar an exaltation from those of the dervish Rumi. He of the 8,000 whirling verses. But, before approaching that mystic condition, one must first accept the diminution of (constructed) self, the dissolution of the personality, that comes with honest admiration. That diminution was something Baudelaire never could accept. That diminution was too high a price, in the end. He would not pay it. Not even though the alternative was madness.

ALEX: I'd like us to end with a poem of his. Have you brought the book?

YAHIA: Yes, I am carrying my copy of "Les Fleurs du Mal."

ALEX: That's still an arrestable offense in some states.

YAHIA: I know it. I'm going to read you his poem called The Albatross. It's a famous poem, and rightly so. Here is the poet before the awful pride carried away his hopes. Here is the poet as misfit and vulnerable. Behold, as Nietzsche wrote, the man!.

Sometimes, to entertain themselves, the men of the crew
Lure upon deck an unlucky albatross, one of those vast
Birds of the sea that follow unwearied the voyage through,
Flying in slow and elegant circles above the mast.

No sooner have they disentangled him from their nets
Than this aerial colossus, shorn of his pride,
Goes hobbling pitiably across the planks and lets
His great wings hang like heavy, useless oars at his side.

How droll is the poor floundering creature, how limp and weak —
He, but a moment past so lordly, flying in state!
They tease him: One of them tries to stick a pipe in his beak;
Another mimics with laughter his odd lurching gait.

The Poet is like that wild inheritor of the cloud,
A rider of storms, above the range of arrows and slings;
Exiled on earth, at bay amid the jeering crowd,
He cannot walk for his unmanageable wings.

This poem, I think, captures the poet and the predicament in the same net. Here is the price—and the peril. The journals say nothing that the spirit-bird of this verse does not soar above, and leave far behind. This verse stands as a tribute to the ravishing, indelible, undeniable, body of what he was able to accomplish during his short time on earth. A belled reminder of his star-graces, after all that subterranean din.

Alex Stein calls poetry "the alphabet zoo."

"We convene on the grounds of the alphabet zoo, and see what there is to see," he says.

"They are all poets," Alex continues. "Nietzsche, too. And Kafka. If the term is to have any meaning at all.

"The true poets, the deep poets, destiny's poets, in prose or verse, madness, eloquence, or silence, are all connected to one another by a mutuality of intention.

"This intention goes by many names, but, fundamentally, it is a rage for transformation."

And then he sighs and quotes Baudelaire. "Anywhere! Just so long as it is out of this world."

Part One: "If my Devils are to leave Me"

I

Yahia: I'd had to set the frail ones aside for a while. They were haunting my mind. All the invalids. Those gilled creatures thrown upon the earth, gasping for a breath from their home atmosphere. I couldn't bear to pity any more suffering. Each one forever on the verge of nervous collapse. I'd combed their letters. I'd inhabited their journals. I'd read between their lines. I didn't want to return to those frailties. I was afraid of what echoing responses they might draw from me.

I imagined them, sometimes, those too-sensitive instruments of reception, vibrating to the wild thunder of some approaching stampede, which is also like the palpitations of an impending panic attack.

Nietzsche. Rilke. Vilhelm Ekelund. As I consider them, now, they appear together almost as one exquisite body. If I had to come up with a single name for this triad, it might be The Exquisites.

Or I might call them The Goners, because all of them are completely gone.

They are The Exquisites by temperament, but they are The Goners because the going for them is all in this world they have to which to cling.

Nietzsche writes, *"existence and the world appear justified only as an aesthetic phenomenon."*

II

YAHIA: Style was important to Nietzsche.

In an aphorism titled, "One Thing is Needful," Nietzsche writes, *"To give style to one's character. A great and rare art. He exercises it who surveys all that his nature presents in strength and weakness and then molds it into an artistic plan, until everything appears as art and reason and even weakness delights the eye."*

In another one, he writes, *"Improving our style means improving our ideas. Nothing less."*

An earlier sculptor of the self, Plotinus put it this way: *"Draw into yourself and look and if you do not find yourself beautiful yet, act as does the creator of a statue that is to be made beautiful. He cuts away here, he smooths there. He makes this line lighter, that one purer. Cut away all the excess. Straighten all that is crooked. Bring light to all that is overcast. Labor to make all one glow or beauty and never cease chiseling your statue..."*

"The style is the man himself," writes George-Louis Leclerc de Buffon.

For Nietzsche, as for Rilke and Ekelund, to write was to cast a spell.

It begins as attention and builds into trance.

It is not so much writing, sometimes, as it is a recovering of the territories lost in what Christianity calls "the fall."

That garden, given us as birthright, from which some

say we were exiled, and others that we simply wandered away.

III

YAHIA: Returning to Nietzsche on this occasion, I am reminded how much he is not what he seems to be. And how much it is he who is to blame for this confusion.

I've been preparing myself for our talk by reading a collection of writings called Conversations with Nietzsche, a few leaves of memory from some few who had spent time with him, spoken with the man himself. If you can believe such a thing possible.

That history lives with us a while, and breathes, before it passes into its own ghost.

Lou Salomé, the woman whom Nietzsche referred to as his "twin soul," was twenty-one when they met. He was thirty-seven.

Nietzsche was smitten like he never had been before and never would be again.

Salomé is particularly constituted to hear Nietzsche, and what she recognizes immediately upon engaging him is his "religious" temperament.

One experienced from him, she writes, the sense *"that he will step forth as the proclaimer of a new religion, and then it will be such a one as recruits heroes to be its disciples."*

Early on in their conversations, Nietzsche confides to

Salomé that he considers himself to be a "tertium quid," which means "a disembodied third person or entity."

It composes, Nietzsche told her. *"I am neither mind nor body…"*

There is never a good time to remind anyone that so-and-so eventually went mad.

Nietzsche spent the last ten years of his life mad.

His last extended act of sanity was his autobiography, Ecce Homo (Behold the Man).

In that autobiography there is a poem which we may call "The Gondola Song."

People forget this, but Nietzsche penned more than a few poems during his tenure as furious world guardian and crisis-hour moralizer.

"And my soul," the poem reads, *"a stringed instrument, / Sang, touched by invisible hands."*

It is this song that bursts from Nietzsche's lips when he has gone mad and is being escorted on a night train to the clinic.

I imagine his escort, a friend who was sent to retrieve him, a sensitive person who believes he is doing a good deed, a service to one troubled beyond bearing by the sight of a world so unashamed of the baseness of its enterprise, a world so shocking with self-deceit, a world so violent.

There is never a good time to mention that Nietzsche may have gone mad from pity.

I imagine the other passengers. There must have been some. Middle class. Tired. Deep within the play of their own private lives. At the sound of his sudden exaltation, inclining slightly toward him.

"And my soul, a stringed instrument, / Sang, touched by invisible hands."

In "Human, All Too Human," Nietzsche had written, *"The most fortunate author is one who is able to say as an old man that all he had of life-giving, invigorating, uplifting, enlightening thoughts and feelings still lives on in his writings, and that he himself is only the gray ash, while the fire has been rescued and carried forth everywhere."*

Is this what had occurred? Is this what the other passengers were witnessing?

And what of the escort? That friend who accompanied him to the end of his genius and through the door of madness.

IV

YAHIA: Nietzsche came up with at least two conceptions almost over-full with crazy wisdom: the Overman and the Eternal Recurrence.

"Man is something that shall be overcome," writes Nietzsche. *"Man is a rope tied between beast and Overman. A rope over an abyss… What is great in man is that he is a bridge and not an end."*

The concept of Eternal Recurrence is a rather astounding idea for an individual to simply encounter. Even an individual of Nietzsche's capacities.

Nietzsche, we can agree, was not a rationalist. Fine, nor is life, nor any other thing, rational. We accept this about Nietzsche, with the genius. But even accepting this, the conception of Eternal Recurrence is still almost too irrational. One would have to be a little crazy in the not-necessarily-romantic sense, one would have to have looked pretty deeply into the abyss, just to think of it, wouldn't one?

And, yet, it is a conception that affirms life in the most profound sense.

Given his context, and knowing his biography and knowing that he had rejected Christianity, and that he had rejected God and the promises of an immortal hereafter, the Eternal Recurrence is Nietzsche's way of sanctifying every day.

It is the big idea that asked of his every action, every day, are you prepared to do this over and over again for eternity?

"What if some day or night a demon were to steal after you in your loneliest loneliness and say to you, 'This life as you now live it, as you have lived it, you will have to live once more and innumerable times more, and there will be nothing new in it, but every pain and every joy and every thought and sigh and everything unutterably small or great in your life will have to return to you, all in the same succession and sequence'... Would you not throw yourself down and gnash your teeth and curse the demon who spoke thus? Or have you once experienced a tremendous moment when you would have answered him, 'You are a god, and never have I heard anything more divine!'"

We know Nietzsche's answer to be the latter. His answer is amor fati. Love of his fate. His answer is yes! Eternally. Yes! With all the loneliness and the suffering.

It was worth it. He is prepared to affirm it. All of it. To celebrate the adventure of the life of the spirit.

Of amor fati, he once wrote, "*A formula for greatness in the human being: That one wants nothing to be different. Not merely to bear what is necessary. Still less to conceal it. But to love it.*"

V

Yahia: The solitude seems to be the key to everything. For Nietzsche, for Rilke, for Ekelund. Solitude enough that they can hear the echo of their longing returning as a concentrated drop, direct from heaven. They want to catch it before it lands, before anything human mixes with it.

These drops, rescued one at a time, are what make for their, frankly, incandescent prose and poetry.

The drops are where the writing comes from and the proof of what they have lived, because each drop glistens with that afterbirth.

Rilke calls poems "experiences."

One direct heartbeat from the body of creation.

VI

Yahia: One more glance over Nietzsche's historic situation before moving on to Rilke.

I do see in Nietzsche the lineage of the Ancient Greeks. And I think he would have seen himself, to a large extent, this way, as an anachronistic Ancient Greek. It's almost a joke that he was not born into that time. He responded so deeply, on so many levels, to the sensibility. There is a paradoxical aphorism that he wrote: *"Oh, those Greeks! They knew how to live. What is required for that is to stop courageously, at the surface, the fold, the skin, to adore appearances, to believe in forms, tones, words and the whole Olympus of appearance. Those Greeks were superficial out of profundity."*

VII

YAHIA: On to Rilke, now, but carrying with us, perhaps, this Greek inheritance.

On Socrates' ladder, the inheritance begins with sexual love, and progresses to the aesthetic appreciation of form in all bodies, and then to the love of beautiful souls, and finally to a contemplation of the ideal form.

In "Archaic Torso of Apollo" (Stephen Mitchell's translation), Rilke writes:

We cannot know his legendary head
with eyes like ripening fruit. And yet his torso
is still suffused with brilliance from inside…
Otherwise…the curved breast could not dazzle you so…
from all the borders of itself…
burst like a star: for here there is no place
that does not see you. You must change your life.

"Boo!" wouldn't have surprised me more, the first time I read the ending, than did "You must change your life."

Here is Rilke, beginning in admiration and ending in

awe. Here is Rilke, a rapt witness in the territory of the sublime. *"That beauty which,.../Hath terror in it"* of which Milton wrote. Fair enough.

Quite a notion, that a human being could realize such a poem.

Though if such a poem were already in one, it would be equally surprising if it could be contained.

VIII

YAHIA: Rilke was another sculptor of the self, always chiseling at his statue, so it makes sense that he fell under the influence of the sculptor Auguste Rodin. This is the ethic that Rodin imparted to Rilke: There is only work.

Rodin also gave Rilke a way to see newly. And his engagement with Rodin coincided with his "thing" poems. Poems in which the "thing" is definite.

In a letter to Lou Andreas-Salomé (the same Salomé who had known Nietzsche, would become Rilke's lover and confidante fifteen years later), Rilke writes, *"The thing is definite, the art thing must be more definite still, removed from all accident, wrested away from all obscurity, withdrawn from time and given over to space. It has become enduring, capable of eternity. The model seems. The art thing is."*

Thanks, at least in part, to Rodin, he is now in a more concrete place.

And it is from this place that "Archaic Torso of Apollo" comes.

This "thing" which is out there stuffed with brilliance from the inside, and gleaming with power, took him. He sent it back, and it returned to him again, this time in the form of transformation.

IX

YAHIA: There is no backing out once you have committed to this project, this self-sculpting, to match yourself to your ideals.

Rilke writes:

Who, if I cried out, would hear me among the angels'
hierarchies? and even if one of them pressed me
suddenly against his heart: I would be consumed
in that overwhelming existence. For beauty is nothing
but the beginning of terror,
which we still are just able to endure,
and we are so awed because it serenely disdains
to annihilate us. Every angel is terrifying.

This is Mitchell's translation of the first passage from the first of the ten beatific Duino Elegies Rilke wrote in a few-weeks' burst of poetic power, in retreat at the Duino castle. And with these elegies, by every standard, Rilke proved himself to himself.

Even five years after the writing of these ten elegies, he was content to play mage, to compose his endless, gorgeous, crystalline letters of instruction, of elucidation, of connection. The letters were his pleasure, because he had gotten the fire out of himself.

He sang his song and he is now the ash.

Not unhappy to be ash for the last five years of his life, is how one might describe it. There is a sense in Rilke of having achieved, and that achievement was not so much the deed of composition as it was the achievement of being ready, being prepared, being patient, and being willing to let this beauty and terror come through him when the time for it was upon him.

One year before Rilke passed away, he was asked to elaborate on the elegies, which had come to him as lightning comes to a lightning rod.

He begins by speaking on the coexistence of the material and the spiritual realms.

"It was within the power of the creative artist to build a bridge between two worlds, even though the task was almost too great for a man. Everywhere transience is plunging into the depths of Being. It is our task to imprint this temporary, perishable earth into ourselves, so deeply, so painfully and passionately, that its essence can rise again, invisible, inside of us. We are the bees of the invisible. We wildly collect the honey of the visible, store it in the great golden hive of the invisible."

X

Yahia: I must now go on immediately to Ekelund.

Vilhelm Ekelund was a literary soul-gazer.

In an aphorism, he writes, "*There are passages in the works of some authors that in a way lie outside the frame of their writing. Passages where you suddenly feel the man talking is not the literary worker So-and-So, but the human being high above all 'literature.' Clear, deep, good—but also with a wild tone, flying through the soul, like the scream of a bird above a desolate ocean bay.*"

XI

Yahia: Rilke writes: "*Space reaches from us and construes the world. / To know a tree in its true element, / throw inner-space around it, from that pure / abundance in you.*"

The Exquisites all cultivated these exquisite states, in order to intensify their inwardness and access the numinous.

That's just something I thought worth mentioning.

Ekelund writes: "*How did I become a hunter for treasure? When I saw a climate (a land) in my nature, in the traditions of my blood which was my heritage. Then I began to realize that the strife of my whole existence was this: to prove my right to inherit...*"

Ekelund is a discovery I owe to the Swedish poet Boel Schenlaer, whom I met at an international festival. I was raving about Nietzsche and the aphorism, presumptively, as it turned out. "You must read Ekelund," she insisted.

I understood why immediately upon opening the first book. The way you know immediately upon meeting certain people.

Ekelund was born in 1880 (Nietzsche was still around then) and died in 1949. He began as a poet, and a gifted, accomplished poet, so that by twenty-three years of age he was considered Sweden's foremost poet. Then, being the radical temperament that he must have been, to keep company, as I see it, with the other Exquisites, he renounced poetry as sentimental and did not publish any more verse.

He practiced a kind of literary soul-gazing. *"Books must be lived to be read,"* he writes. He saw into the writers he read in ways that others don't. He composed essays and aphorisms.

He discovered Nietzsche at twenty-seven. He turned to Nietzsche *"for learning, strength and solace."*

Nietzsche taught him that it is possible to be a great poet of ideas writing in prose.

By his forties, Ekelund wrote exclusively in aphorisms.

The aphorism integrates both existential and moral commitment, and that is what Ekelund was after. No less!

Ekelund writes: *"An even accumulation of divine sunshine, slow and blissful, no artist's fever with repercussions of tumbling into darkness. My worship of the sun begins in the autumn, culminates in February.*"

Ekelund writes: "*The real poet is a mystic.*"

Ekelund would not write for money and lived sometimes in the most heartbreaking poverty. He tied a rope around his waist for a belt and slept as a vagrant. He led a terrible life and desperate.

He didn't have Rilke's gift for cultivating princesses and baronesses.

He collapsed with a lung ailment and was in recovery when he wrote "The Second Light."

As he was recovering, he began to hear himself breathe, and with that awareness his breath changed altogether.

He was quieted somehow.

Nietzsche had advised that no thoughts could be trusted but those that came to one while walking.

Ekelund, who would never stop thinking, took this advice for his medicine.

Aerial Photographs of a Subterranean Labyrinth

"There are some writers," says Yahia, "in whom one can see one's own possibilities. And that is the relationship one forges with those writers when one engages them. I never could see my own possibilities in Kierkegaard. Not with my eyes open. But, there are two ways to understand. You can understand without knowing how you understand and you can understand knowing precisely how you understand. Understanding with the eyes closed and understanding with the eyes open. I never could understand Kierkegaard with my eyes open. He was too many, too much, too elusive. Where was his core self? It wasn't until I realized that at his core was a ball of molten poetry that I was finally able to see him, and with him, myself. Whatever else he was or wasn't, he was a great poet of the ideal, of longing, of obsession. I had already understood Kierkegaard with my eyes closed. The way for example if one were asked to explain a certain poem one wouldn't even know where to start, only that some great spoon had stirred one to the depths. I had understood Kierkegaard all along with my eyes closed, but now I knew the earth of him, around which the many moons revolved."

I

Alex: What do you suppose, in Søren Kierkegaard, is the well-spring of all that sorrow?

YAHIA: The best place to begin is with his biography. There are two people to whom Kierkegaard dedicates his writing. His father, who as an eight-year-old child laborer, hungry, angry and deprived, cursed God from a mountain-top, and 70 years later still could not forget it or forgive himself, is one. And Regina Olsen, whom Kierkegaard drags into immortality having abandoned her in the world, is the other.

These relationships can't answer for everything. At the end there will still be question marks weaving riddles above his head and question marks etched like a tribal scarring into his broad pale brow. But these are two places where one can reasonably begin.

The father sires seven children, only two of whom outlive him, Søren and older brother Peter. The father believes this is part of God's retribution against his inexpiable sin.

Thus, young Søren is raised in an atmosphere of metaphysical gloom and ever-present guilt, in the shadow of a father who believes there is nothing for which he can hope, neither in this world, nor in the next.

But this same father also gets Kierkegaard's imagination going. Father and son don't get out much, but the father often escorts young Søren around their home as if along a busy town thoroughfare. There they encounter imaginary men and women and dodge imaginary clattering carriages and see brilliant imaginary sights.

It is on this thoroughfare, to a large extent, that Kierkegaard remains.

'*Humanly speaking, I was insanely raised,*' Kierkegaard will later write.

Accounts of Søren Kierkegaard, by people who knew him across the gamut of his years, describe him as gregarious, thoroughly charming, and wholly lovable. A child with children. A wit with the witty. He cultivated gaiety, but also a kind of intimate immediacy, and presented himself around Copenhagen as sociable in the extreme.

Privately he would lapse into periods of brooding and melancholy.

These he kept hidden.

But, how wondrous those lapses must have been. Filled with the extraordinary ordinary experiences of a self in the process of re-creating into a world literary figure and matchless philosopher. And filled too with his gift for the play of spirits in a theater of the gods.

The other important part of Kierkegaard's biography is his engagement to Regina Olsen.

Olsen is ten years Kierkegaard's junior when they meet. She is 14. He is at a friend's home where she is taking piano lessons.

Unrealistic, romantic, as Kierkegaard is, he knows well enough to wait until she is 16 before declaring his devotion. "*Since I first laid eyes on you,*" he tells Olsen, "*I knew.*"

At once, they are in love and the next moment they are engaged.

A year into this engagement, however, Kierkegaard has a crisis. He determines to himself that he is ill-suited for marriage. He no longer believes it would be ethical to drag another person into the inward life to which he believes he has been called.

He doesn't want Olsen to feel rejected, so he tries every indirect method his febrile mind can conjure to provoke in Olsen a realization that she would be better off without him. He presents himself as a cad, aloof, cruel—the opposite of what he really is.

She loves him unceasingly.

Her father tries reason. *"You mustn't,"* he insists. *"Regina will harm herself. She believes in you so deeply."*

"Is there someone else?" Olsen will finally have to ask. *"Will there be someone else? Is that why you wish to leave me?"*

At the end of his nuance, his delicacy, his generosity, Kierkegaard will reply, *"Maybe not now, but in ten years time, I may want some young girl to fan the flames of my lust again."*

After the broken engagement has become official, Kierkegaard retreats to the cloister of a wholly interior life. He has chosen duty over happiness. This is his one true failing. He does not believe there is enough room in his life for both.

Olsen lingers in Kierkegaard's mind as he writes, a symbol, a token, a medal of valor from his brief stint in worldly life, spurring his insight, his dialectical intensity, his fantastical mask-making, and his critical ingenuity.

He never imagines her to marry, but she does marry.

Maybe he had thought that because he made the sacrifice, she would be returned to him the way faithful Abraham's son Isaac is spared and returned to Abraham.

But, Olsen's marriage, to the philosopher Friedrich Schlegel, is a good one.

Olsen is bright eyed with her dull but perfectly kind and thoughtful husband.

Kierkegaard, at age 42, a bachelor, esteemed in his lifetime as the greatest religious thinker Denmark has ever produced (several thousand people attend his Church funeral) gets to dead, after first dropping in the street and being taken to a hospital.

He has not much money left. He had been living on an allowance from his father, who after that impoverished childhood, came into a modest income.

It is even said that he had just taken the last of that allowance money out of trust on the day he fell in the street. And it was with that last money that he paid his hospital stay.

In the room he left behind, there was a locked drawer and in that drawer there were two envelopes addressed to his brother Peter, a local priest, with whom Kierkegaard had a strained relationship.

One can imagine the competition for the father's graces making this sibling connection almost impossible from the start.

One can imagine the one who had become a priest being more of a reassurance to the guilt stricken father, than the one who had become something more like a religious jester.

One can imagine, too, the genius of Kierkegaard as he might have been from a pulpit. God, what an opportunity was lost to history when he was not simply ceded an honorary divinity certificate and offered a local Copenhagen parish.

One of the envelopes contains Kierkegaard's will. In it Kierkegaard asserts that even though he and Olsen were only engaged he takes that engagement just as seriously as though they had married.

Everything, including all of his writings, go to Olsen.

"The one unnamed, whose name some day will be named," he writes, *"to whom all my work is dedicated, is my erstwhile fiancée Regina Schlegel."*

A year or so afterwards, Olsen will enter into a correspondence with Kierkegaard's nephew, a hot-blooded, passionate type, not too different from Kierkegaard in some ways, who had been the one who tended Kierkegaard during his last days alive.

"You say he mentioned me when he lay ill," Olsen will write. *"I do so much want to know what he said."*

According to the nephew, what the uncle said was: *"I have my thorn in the flesh, like Paul. Hence, I could not be like other folk, so I concluded my task was to be the extraordinary. It was this that was the hindrance with Regina. I had believed it could be changed, but it could not, so I broke the engagement."*

Maudlin, if he did say it. But, maudlin or not, it would echo things he had said all along: *"I am the corrective. I am the exception. I am the pinch of spice needed to impart a particular taste to the rest."*

Elsewhere he refers to *"Some missed relationship between soul and body."* Elsewhere he refers to: *"My silent despair."*

In the same letter, Olsen had also written, *"I feel I have shirked a duty through cowardice. A duty not only toward Søren, but toward God to whom he sacrificed me. Whether he did this (as he himself sometimes thought might be the case) through an in-born tendency to self-torture, or as I take it that time and the results of his activities have shown, through an inner call from God."*

II

It is impossible for me not to be delighted with the vision of Søren Kierkegaard on the streets of Copenhagen, full of mischief, full of delight. A kinder, more ethereal, Socrates.

III

The poet Auden who wrote of Rilke that Rilke was *"the greatest lesbian poet since Sappho,"* also wrote that Kierkegaard sometimes carried on *"like a spiritual prima-donna."*

IV

Søren Kierkegaard was able to treat the streets of

Copenhagen as a large reception room in which to play at life. He wrote of being able to enter into rapprochement with anyone he chose, just by hooking that person with his eyes.

Hans Brockner, a friend, a distant relative, an atheist philosopher, witness to this side of the man, writes of a meeting he had with Kierkegaard in the streets, shortly after Kierkegaard's return from Berlin where he had sequestered himself after the broken engagement, writing with his mind aflame.

"He spoke of my doings and studies and told me that in Berlin he had longed for many things, among which was to see me. He could say such things with a characteristically winning expression. His smile and his look were expressive to a degree difficult to describe. He had a way of greeting one at a distance with a look. It was only a little movement of the eye and yet the expression meant so much. There was at times something infinitely gentle and loving in his look, but also something goading. He was able with a glance to put himself "en rapport" with a passer-by, as he expressed it. Anyone meeting that glance was either attracted or else repelled. Made embarrassed, uncertain."

"I was once walking through a whole street with him while he explained how one can make psychological studies by so putting oneself en-rapport to passers-by and as he explained his theory he put it in practice with almost everyone we met. There was no one on whom his glance did not make an obvious impression."

V

"What this age needs is not a genius," writes Kierkegaard, *"but a martyr who in order to teach men to obey would himself be obedient unto death. What this age needs is awakening and therefore someday not only my writings but my whole life, all the intriguing mystery of the machine will be studied and studied."*

VI

Kierkegaard wants to figure out what to do. He is so wildly alive in the world of potentialities. It is only in the world of actualities that he is still-born. He is never quite able to commit. Forget Regina Olsen! She's a great symbol, obviously. But, even without that example, what did Kierkegaard ever commit to, except the one thing he did commit to?

Inwardness. The life of the spirit.

From early on he is asking himself: What is to be my mission?

He is not of the disposition to make things easier.

"Talk to me of justice," Socrates says to the learned judge he stops on the streets of Athens. *"You are the person of law. Help me to understand what justice is."*

The learned must be made to understand how little they have of learning before the true understanding can commence.

"It was intelligence and nothing else that had to be opposed," Kierkegaard wrote. *"Presumably that is why I who had the job was armed with an immense intelligence."*

You asked me, "What is the well-spring of Kierkegaard's sorrow?"

I must answer that I don't believe anyone can live happily against his own nature.

VII

Kierkegaard's nature is an analytical one. He's an excellent candidate for a debate team. He's such a great debater. If he decides, for his life's task, to oppose intelligence, there is already something in that formulation that is quite tragic.

VIII

I can understand how the critical mind is an impediment. Always interfering and deciphering.

IX

However Kierkegaard disparaged the aesthetic life as one of the early stages, preceding the ethical and the religious, in many ways the aesthetic was his domain. It was his great stage in the sense too of a performance space. The aesthetic works were truer (however less exalted and sublime they seemed to him) on a simple level, and even on a very complex level, to who he was.

X

Toward the end of his life, Kierkegaard comes out as a Christian writer. He is no longer hiding. He is no longer playing games. He is no longer sounding through a mask. He believes he is speaking for Christianity.

I think of this Wilde line: *"Give a man a mask and he'll tell you the truth."*

XI

The conflict of being an extraordinarily intelligent human being who is at war with his own intelligence.

XII

Just shy of 40, Kierkegaard writes: *"Our literature in this century has shown an almost abnormal richness in poetry. Our prose on the contrary has declined. We lacked a prose which bore the stamp of artistry. This lack I have supplied and this is why my writings will retain their importance in literature."*

This is the craftsman who knows it is not just what he says but how he says it.

XIII

No one can help us develop inwardness. Certainly no church. That would just be more hollow externals.

Kierkegaard's inwardness was complicated because it led to brooding introspection which led to despair.

But it was also despair which led to brooding introspection which led to the inwardness.

XIV

Kierkegaard writes of the "jammed lock" of inwardness. The despair that doesn't lead to eternity. That paralyzes, cripples.

XV

When Regina Olsen gets the news that Kierkegaard has willed her his worldly estate, her response, after consultation with her husband, is to politely demur. Olsen asks only that a few personal effects be returned.

The ideal works in poetry. It works in the aesthetic realm. But when these standards are applied to ordinary life, they are bound to fail.

XVII

"It's really not worth bothering oneself with men," writes Kierkegaard, *"except with those who have given their life for something or at least have religious or desperate energy enough to think of death every day."*

XVIII

One of the first things his father disapproves of early on, when Kierkegard is in his 20s, is his attraction to German Romanticism.

Young Søren is meant to study theology, to study philosophy.

But it is the poets to whom he responds.

He prefers the thorn to the rose.

Acknowledgements

Conversations with Nietzsche: A Life in the Words of His Contemporaries Sander L. Gilman (Editor), David J. Parent (Translator) Oxford University Press, USA (June 20, 1991) | *Rimbaud: Complete Works, Selected Letters, a Bilingual Edition* Arthur Rimbaud, Seth Whidden (Editor), Wallace Fowlie (Translator) University Of Chicago Press; Revised edition (November 1, 2005) | *The Basic Kafka*, Franz Kafka, Pocket Books (June 3, 1984) | *Papers and Journals: A Selection*, Søren Kierkegaard, Alastair Hannay (Editor, Translator) Penguin Classics (November 1, 1996) | *The Picture of Dorian Gray and Three Stories*, Oscar Wilde, Tribeca Books (December 7, 2010) | *The Portable Nietzsche* Friedrich Nietzsche, Walter Kaufmann (Translator) Penguin Books (January 27, 1977) | *Nietzsche: Volumes One and Two*, Martin Heidegger, HarperOne (March 1, 1991) | *Aphorisms*, Franz Kafka, Michael Hofmann and Geoffrey Brock (Translators), Roberto Calasso (Editor) Schocken (December 26, 2006) | *Conversations with Kafka*, Gustav Janouch, Goronwy Rees (Translator), Francine Prose (Introduction) New Directions (January 26, 2012) | *On Nietzsche*, Georges Bataille, Paragon House (August 27, 1998) | *Intimate Journals*, Charles Baudelaire, Christopher Isherwood (Translator), W. H. Auden (Introduction) Dover Publications (June 16, 2006) | *The Waste Land and Other Writings*, T.S. Eliot, Mary Karr (Introduction) Modern Library (January 8, 2002) | *Selected Prose of T. S. Eliot*,T. S. Eliot, Frank Kermode (Editor) Mariner Books (November 10, 1975) | *Les Fleurs Du*

Mal, (English and French Edition) Charles Baudelaire, Richard Howard (Translator) David R. Godine (October 1, 1985) | *New and Collected Poems: 1931-2001*, Czeslaw Milosz, Ecco (March 25, 2003) | *The Selected Poetry of Rainer Maria Rilke*, (English and German Edition) Rainer Maria Rilke (Author), Stephen Mitchell (Editor, Translator), Robert Hass (Introduction) Vintage (March 13, 1989) | *Letters of Rainer Maria Rilke, 1910-1926*, Rainer Maria Rilke, Jane Bannard Greene and M.D. Herter Norton (Translators) W. W. Norton & Company (January 1st 1948) | *The Second Light*, Vilhelm Ekelund, Lennart Bruce (Translator), Eric O. Johannesson (Afterword) North Point Press (1986) | *Parables of Kierkegaard*, Søren Kierkegaard, Thomas C. Oden (Editor) Princeton University Press (September 1, 1989) | *Encounters with Kierkegaard: a life as seen by his contemporaries*, Collected, edited, and annotated by Bruce H. Kirmmse, Bruce H. Kirmmse and Virginia R. Laursen (Translators) Princeton University Press (1996) |

Our gratitude to the fine editors of the following journals who first published these works: The Prayer of Attention, *Agni, 2010* | Aerial Photographs of a Subterranean Labyrinth, *The Pinch, 2011* | The Exquisites, *Agni, 2011* | It Could Have Been Otherwise, *The Literary Review, 2011* | To Go and Seek the Twilight Hour, *Gulf Coast Review, 2011* |

www.ingramcontent.com/pod-product-compliance
Lightning Source LLC
LaVergne TN
LVHW050939080826
845145LV00004B/1331

* 9 7 8 0 9 8 7 2 7 6 0 4 9 *